Princess Puzzles

Stella Maidment and Daniela Dogliani

Editor: Alexandra Koken
Designer: Elaine Wilkinson

Copyright © QED Publishing 2012

First published in the UK in 2012 by
QED Publishing
A Quarto Group company
230 City Road
London EC1V 2TT

www.qed-publishing.co.uk

A catalogue record for this book is available
from the British Library.

ISBN 978 1 84835 863 8

Printed in China

If you get stuck, the answers are at the back of the book!

Welcome to the Palace!

This is the king.

This is the queen.

This is Princess Pearl!

Solve the puzzles in this book and help Pearl find a friend.

Look out for Alphonso the cat as well. You'll find him in every picture!

Princess Pearl lives
in a very big palace.

She's in her bedroom in the tallest tower. Can you find her?

Can you spot these things?

two horses

three white birds

a flag

5

Pearl's playroom is filled with toys and games.

Can you spot these things?

two dinosaurs

a drum

a pink rabbit

Can you find four differences between the two teddies?

Pearl's dressing room is filled with beautiful clothes.

Can you match her shoes to her dresses?

Can you spot these things?

a blue necklace

a golden chair

a crown

There are lots of lovely things
to do in the palace garden.

Can you spot
these things?

three
butterflies

a scooter

a watering can

Can you help Pearl find her way to the swing?

There's just one thing missing:
Pearl has no one to play with!

One of the baby swans is different
from the others. Which one?

Can you spot these things?

three red flowers

two statues

a frog

On Pearl's birthday, the king and queen give her lots of presents.

Can you spot these things?

a blue and yellow present

a book

two birthday cards

Follow Pearl's ribbon to find her favourite present.

Pearl still wishes she had a friend to play with.

Then she notices a door she's never seen before.

Can you spot these things?

three paintings

a suit of armour

a mouse

The door is small and green. Can you find it?

Pearl opens the door and sees some stairs. They lead to the palace kitchen!

Can you spot these things?

 an ironing board

three lamps

a crate of apples

Help Pearl find
her way there.

19

Tilly, the cook's daughter, is helping to make Pearl's birthday cake.

Can you spot these things?

a kettle

two baskets

a clock

Can you find the outlines of a knife, a fork and a spoon hidden in this picture?

21

Pearl puts on a stripy apron and joins in. Baking is lots of fun!

Can you see three
more stripy things?

Can you spot
these things?

a recipe
book

a loaf of
bread

butter

Afterwards, Tilly and Pearl play with Pearl's new puppet theatre.

Can you spot these things?

three red stars

three puppets

a toy panda

Can you guess what their show is called?

Pearl has found a friend at last!
"This is my best birthday ever!"
she says.

HAPPY

Can you spot
these things?

Alphonso's
new friend!

three pink
cakes

a red jelly

Answers

Pages 4-5

Pearl is circled in red.

Pages 6-7

The four differences are circled in red.

Pages 8-9

Follow the lines to match up the shoes and dresses.

Pages 10-11

Follow the red line to the swing.

Pages 12-13

Alphonso

The baby swan circled in red looks different.

Pages 14-15

Alphonso

Pearl's ribbon (highlighted in red) leads to the puppet theatre.

Pages 16-17

Alphonso

The small green door is circled in red.

Pages 18-19

Alphonso

Follow the red line to the palace kitchen.

Answers

The three outlines are circled in red.

The three other stripy things are circled in red.

Pages 24-25

The show is called 'Little Red Riding Hood'.

Pages 26-27

The matching balloons are circled in red.

More princess fun

Princess day
Dress up as a princess for the day! Put on a pretty dress and see if you can borrow some necklaces or bracelets to wear. Use a towel for a cloak and tape or safety pin it onto your dress. You could even have a princess-themed party!

Put on a show!
You can put on a puppet show just like Pearl and Tilly! Cut out pictures of people or animals from magazines and stick them on the ends of chopsticks, wooden spoons or sticks from the park. Hide behind a sofa and hold your puppets up so they peep out over the top. Then let the puppet show begin!

Make a jewelled crown
Find a strip of coloured paper that's long enough to wrap around your head, then cut a zig-zag edge along the top. To make 'jewels', cut out circles or diamonds from foil or cellophane wrappers. Now glue the shapes onto the crown to decorate it. When you are finished, glue or tape the ends of the crown together.

Make a royal castle
Draw an outline of a castle on a piece of paper. Use paints, crayons or pencils to colour it in. Then draw a king, a queen and a princess on separate pieces of paper, cut them out and glue them onto your castle. When you've finished, you can hang your castle picture on the wall!